T0113307

MIGHTY

RANDOM 2

Asha Bianca

WESTBOW
PRESS®
A DIVISION OF THOMAS NELSON
& ZONDERVAN

WestBow Press books may be ordered through
booksellers or by contacting:

WestBow Press
A Division of Thomas Nelson & Zondervan
1663 Liberty Drive
Bloomington, IN 47403
www.westbowpress.com
1 (866) 928-1240

ISBN: 978-1-5127-5248-9 (sc)

Print information available on the last page.

WestBow Press rev. date: 10/28/2016

RANDOM THOUGHTS FROM THE WEEK:

Those rowing the boat generally don't rock it.

Communicate.

Be silent.

Know your timing.

Started using an email folder "fun" @ work. Good thinking.

Best explanation I've ever heard for thunder and lightning - God is playing a concert. Thunder is drums and lightning is the flash of all the cameras taking His picture while he's playing! - T.

Some days just need to stop.

March madness my 1st bracket, pretty proud!

Really you're going to pick Oregon after all you put California through - e to me.

Hot showers in Wisconsin and cold showers in Haiti, got-it.

Flying to California on this windy Wednesday night, magic!

Remember to shave your legs.

Fast.

Pray.

Tree huggers unite.

Folks in pain.

Key 2 traveling, take one leg at a time, don't get ahead of yourself, enjoy the journey.

Woods heal, I knew it, Tara confirmed.

Present 2 a CEO or General, toss-up.

Talent is attractive.

Remember where you came from.

Boarding soon, Peace out.

Beach.

RANDOM THOUGHTS FROM THE WEEK:

help others be accountable.

It's easier to clean together, both rooms and pasts.

Long hugs in the hallway & the kitchen.

Stop asking why.

See a sunrise on a Saturday.

Cashton.

When you know the barista @ Starbucks.

Variety is the spice of life, add some cinnamon.

7am, kids outside on their swing set in Bangor, good time.

People in farm towns rarely sleep-in.

Find your great.

Fresh curds.

Piggyback rides in the middle of a park.

Know the weight of your words.

Encouragement from Momma Nanc <3.

day 1 T let the pups out so I didn't miss any games, day 2 T built a bookshelf for E while I was at church, good record so far.

Mother Teresa's footprints.

Sometimes when Sol seems very hungry he is just chucking pomegranate seeds and green peas in aunties backseat.

spring forward is rough on Mondays.

Go to Haiti.

Mookie.

Pumpkin, rhubarb and peach - only on pie day.

I love Ethan's exuberant yes when I ask if he wants me to cook him meat :) all boy.

Might of caught a teapot on fire while engrossed in conversation with my sis. Just love her so.

Having a Hawaiian calendar may not be the best idea. Tried to jump in a page 2day.

I so want a redo 4 nap day! No nap = not right.

Chels is there 4 my dad, no words <3.

RANDOM THOUGHTS FROM THE WEEK:

Take the tub.

Forget to shave your legs.

Buy the shirt.

Let yourself off the hook once in a while.

Be diligent.

Psalm 18:30, flawless.

Eagles remind me of Matt.

Eliminate mundane meetings.

The stars are beautiful.

Be brave.

It's interesting how little we actually need.

There is no "g" in fishin'.

Smart people can be wrong.

Boundaries are what's ok and what's not.

Stay in blessed mode.

Do it with all your <3.

3 hours can seem like forever or no time at all, depending on the company you keep.

Camping, camping all I want 2 do is go camping.

The woods should never be "closed", find another forest adventure.

Eat well and mindfully.

California, E and me, 4 more 2morrows. Oh my loves!

I miss Audi, <3.

Study nature. Pray together.

Chels, sweet good night call @ 11 last night, lovely.

Milan.

Hope 4 yourself and others. They may be doing the best they possibly can do, you'll never know.

Give benefit of doubt.

E - 3 game tourney today, oh yeah, can't even wait, bonus time is da best!

Think BIG.

Spring forward.

RANDOM THOUGHTS FROM THE WEEK:

Assess the situation accurately.

When you FaceTime your friend and her table is full of homemade spaghetti and her children, it is wonderful.

Deuteronomy 6: 4-9.

Divine moments happen, especially at barn dances.

If he's dreamy but doesn't show-up for you, he's not dreamy.

After 3 wild wonderful boys, some times you get a girl, these are good times.

Don't steal the ball from your own teammate, good principle in play or at work.

Jenny came and sat by me in the gym, we laughed and caught up, it blessed me.

If you don't want to eat every cookie by yourself, open the box of thin mints during youth group.

Health class doll, so distracting.

Thursday, 7:40am, me and the gym, just us, not another soul. Got it done.

"The victory that culture has gained at the expense of Nature must not be surrendered or given up at any price." Goethe via Gide, mouth and mind full.

Be the boss of you.

When you're really glad you bought the small vs. large bag of chocolate covered cinnamon pretzels from Finnottes because somehow they're all gone...

Be honorable, especially in the tough stuff.

Friends makes me laugh all the time....phoebe...Ross.. Joey...chandler...Rachel...monica...<3

Somm & CFA, similarities.

Felt anger and woe is me for like an hour this morning, what a waste of time, onward.

Mom's illustrations came for book 2, cool.

Friday night, Wonder Woman absent. Be back 2morrow.

Sure do love you.

New day, Be thankful.

Forgot how much I love the show chopped, thanks again chels.

My brother's poem makes me smile...

Birds chirping to call spring forward.

RANDOM THOUGHTS FROM THE WEEK:

Do life big.

I belong in the woods.

Read the entire email.

Dance.

Good friends stand in front of large rodents named Igor with you.

Wee jar of Nutella.

Pig with max and e is a hoot. Buckets 4 days...

When you realize you will see your daughter, dad, dear friends and ocean in 2 weeks, it becomes difficult to keep your mind!

Good morning video from baby girl Ainsley made my year.

Leap!

Bull dog stuff for Knox because she loves them so.

4 inches on March 1, winter part 2 as it is fondly called.

Pray hardest when it's hardest to pray.

Hold hands hiking.

Chelsea is growing up every day, so proud of her, can't even describe it!

When E says, "pack my lunch the exact same as yesterday", my heart smiles.

Sometimes emoticons say it all.

Premier life insurance category, same as Olympic athlete, I'll take it.

Respect is beautiful.

When someone is on your <3, call them.

King of my heart, never gonna let me down.

Play nice.

RANDOM THOUGHTS FROM THE WEEK:

We are not defined by our mess.

The elephant & piggy book series <3

Resist Go Fever.

People notice when you bring Starbucks into Caribou.

Eagles fishing in the Mississippi, love.

Listen, don't natter.

Road trips rock!

Good date etiquette - When he fills your gas tank and checks under your hood just to make sure it is a-ok.

Trout creek road.

Time > $.

Heart in Hawaii.

People you love never really leave your side!

Objective observer.

Fried green tomatoes.

How do you go from jungle book to mexico?

Distance is hard on memorial days and other days too.

Two church services and one hike = a good day.

I will go to that barn dance 1 day.

We have no idea the pain people have been through, let them have their moment.

Dominoes.

There are some good ideas in all minds, seek them out.

Rainbow in Kona.

There is no shame in being a broken man (or woman). Begin again and have faith.

RANDOM THOUGHTS FROM THE WEEK:

Interdependency.

If you look hard enough, you can always find the gold in people.

Empathy - not always agreeing, acknowledging.

Encourage your child to be real.

I hike better in a certain green vest, feel hugged.

Reciprocity.

birthday parties are fun, whether 7 or 75.

Beautiful & healthy Size 16 on cover of SI, not too shabby.

Trust and thankfulness.

Linsanity, watching the Jeremy Lin story with my boy, love it!

40 degrees never felt so good, nothing like the sunshine!

Rooted in the word.

Be interested, don't try 2b interesting.

Ran outside today with buddy boy, oh how I love that pup.

Missions will wreck you - It's a good thing.

E no school, love him relaxing.

Know yourself to lead yourself.

Blue sky, honey Dijon chips, water, Mac and cheese, chicken nuggets - e's co-op asks.

Don't hide insecurities, tell them the truth & move on.

There are really only 3 kinds of people, those who return their carts to the cart corral, those who leave their carts in the parking lot, and those who look for someone walking in who may need a cart.

Buy flowers 4 a stranger who was extra kind, drop them anonymously @ their work with a thank you.

Lean against a tree and dream your world of dreams.... love my dad.

I am.

Wind and spirit mean the same in the Greek, coincidence I think not.

Stuff happens, learn from it.

Care.

Headed to youth, Whoohoo.

Mountains are gorgeous.

Mugby pit stop.

Community of learners working to make a better world.

Sometimes you just have to make your own trail.

Say I forgive you and let it lie.

Thy kingdom come.

Let go and play.

Men & women of mercy, the goal, tougher than it looks folks!

E doesn't miss a beat.

Talk less, listen more.

Be petrified wood not drift wood.

Bitterness keeps you from flying.

Stay humble and kind.

Billie Sue lives and loves big everyday, my coconut bracelet from Haiti is magic!

Newark bound, one day, I think I can...ok, let's roll.

Chels & Kyle, love them so.

Thankful for extra warm clothes in my truck, just in case.

Love notes are best written on birch.

We all have a little goofball in us.

Praying.

RANDOM THOUGHTS FROM THE WEEK:

Come to play, life's too short to be a spectator.

Smile everyday, at least once.

One day this week, after dropping Ethan off @ school, my arms drove straight home instead of 2 work. Lol, it was funny, those wishful thinking arms.

Yoozers = good, got it!

Heart shaped pans bring inspiration.

Where there's a will there's a way, leadership conference, Avett, sweet Lin baby girl & mommas day <3.

Sunrises and sunsets are magic.

I'm having a red cinnamon heart kind of day....4u kyle.

Joe and Wen call, greatest honor.

Even more unreasonable than one could imagine, oh well, done with that. Onward!

I love sea turtles.

Do not calumniate, ever.

Sometimes we're called to peace and sometimes to fight, I am familiar with the former, the latter is stretching my faith. No longer a slave song again & again.

Dance parties with Christmas lights.

I notice when I spend more time substantially praying throughout the day I worry less about the routine of praying over meals.

Not much of a groggery frequenting girl.

Norwegian fish tacos, yum!

Speak truth.

I blocked so and so, well I forget why but it was definitely for a good reason, chels cracks me up!

If you want the inside scoop of what is going on at your son's basketball game, invite an athletic director who makes you smile & shows you the ropes :).

Friendship is a sheltering tree.

Love wins.

RANDOM THOUGHTS FROM THE WEEK:

Good people call your cell when your lights are off.

Feb 2 - first shovel day 4 me, not too shabby. Thank you highlander.

Don't do drugs, even if you don't start out weird, you'll end up weird.

Put your windshield wipers up.

Calm your desiderata.

Friday! Oh how I love Fridays :)

I ate a carton of blueberries this morning.

When you say you'll visit, do.

Going to anyone other than the source is nugatory.

I'm not intimidated by cops, I'm a good guy.

Lunch @ the charmont with Jess is a dream.

Not sure why but I feel calmer getting my inbox to 2,500 instead of 2,530, such a nerd, lol.

Nightmares are scary.

White as snow.

I want 2 eat a makers donut.

Treasure hunt, 13, <3 Abs.

The ref called my purple boots team sponsored.

If you need a heating pad and banana, Barb's house is the spot.

Peoples lives are often more complicated than 1 sees upon 1st glance.

E & me enjoy a good car wash & church service together.

I know he loves you but does he like you, great line.

Revenant - worth the watch, crazy cool imagery!

Don't be a level 10 weenie, yep my pastors says this, and I love it!

Fix your eyes, finish the race.

RANDOM THOUGHTS FROM THE WEEK:

Facetiming.

Create space from someone who tells you not to worry your pretty little head, who you work with. Remember you are paid in part to worry your pretty little head at work.

Moses is bat man.

Funny the way it is.

Shelve some things for the nonce and move on.

Skiing while being pulled by a cowboy on a horse, okay!

Fig Newton fan.

Roast beef and a bloedow's raspberry filled donut is actually a delicious combination.

Proverbs 12:26, choose your circle carefully.

Ultrasound pics are a sneak peek at a miracle.

You know so many people, I mean really know them. I'm not great at small talk.

God heals.

Everyone except you and (blank) know how amazing you are. I love Audi.

Snow day.

My fashion style is to lose one of my earrings, all the time!

I often wear my rainbow skirt on snow days, kinda fun.

Snow shoveling = fast way 2 get warm.

Embrace your roots.

Some days are dark, lighten them together.

Listen to others talk about their dreams.

Watch the MI game with E, if they lose, he may be sad, it's ok.

August 25th, Chels & Kyle <3

RANDOM THOUGHTS FROM THE WEEK:

Other side of the rainbow may not have gold but the journey is golden.

Amish buggies make my day.

If my face doesn't instantly hurt when I walk outside, it's a warm day. Wisconsin gauge.

Bright - echosmith.

Sometimes past team members find you in a cottage, while on their husband's business trip. They give you a hug and you smile.

Eagles fishing on the Mississippi.

Baby girls eyes like her mommas....miracle.

Worst part of getting to work later than 7, parking.

Slow down.

Makers gotta make.

If you're settling, stop.

Focus on God.

Money is the least expensive part of me.

I remember thinking when bringing babies home from the hospital, really I get to keep them forever, nothing like that love!!

Call control's bluff and forget what your insecurities say you can't do, choose faith instead and get 2 work.

Berries are my new favorite road trip snack.

Sometimes I'm just over a song.

Not the first time I've been called a utility player.

Moulin rouge on the big screen, T is kind.

Doesn't matter how long I live here, quite doubtful I will ever drive my vehicle on hard water even though ice fishing is definitely in my future!

E home in t minus five hours, Whoohoo!

Uffda button for Barb.

When Nikole asks how I am, she means it, love this.

Take pups out.

Makes me smile when abs tags me in an Instagram.

The mint 2 go.

Loving life.

RANDOM THOUGHTS FROM THE WEEK:

Quiet is magic.

My sister makes me the best coffee.

Make the bball game.

Even when you're down by 20, keep your head up.

The scars are on the inside, my brother has a way with words.

The book is not going to write itself.

You're in my top five and you owe me a Coke.

Indy.

Chels <3.

Different destinations, 75 in HI & 25 in WI, hi ho hi ho, 2 work I go. Sending love with mom.

E has my #.

Don't get too comfortable climbing up or down a 60ish foot rock face.

Don't get too comfortable driving in a snow storm for three hours.

We take risks on people everyday, make them calculated.

Sometimes those you think you know surprise you 4 the good, let them.

Watch the movie The Martian, e's a fan.

5,200 attractiveness agenda messages aimed at our youth per year by media, ahhhh- determined 2 help counter this with truth!

Thankful for salt trucks.

When you're intimate with God, you aren't intimidated by man.

The best apology is to change behavior.

Show-up for birthdays of those you love, especially with very short notice!

More love, less hustle.

Thank a farmer.

Had e make his own dinner last night, good 4 him.

New baby girl in this world tomorrow, makes me cry with joy!

Singapore does not have my name on it.

If I'm brave enough to write it, magic happens.

Frisky.

E's Social Studies test @ 1:45 today, pray for it.

Youth tonight, Whoohoo, important.

RANDOM THOUGHTS FROM THE WEEK:

Sometimes I drink pellegrino from the bottle.

E's guns though, so muscly, what in the world?

Always say yes to a rock climbing, flying squirrel and rope course combination.

Salt is the number one flavor enhancer in the world.

A half truth is still a whole lie.

Cherish people.

Good hotel room beds have many pillows.

Work is hard, deep breaths.

Some business trips I am thankful for an empty seat next to me.

Encourage = to impart courage to another.

Love how honest my son is, follow the path of integrity.

Airport security guy called me gorgeous and asked if Ethan was my bodyguard, nice! We said he had to check his guns...lol, it's the little stuff.

You're never wrong to do the right thing. - m. twain, the intern was great.

Gentleman is a great word, even better in 3D.

Say your sorry when you are.

Chelsea's party is not a party it's a wedding, never call it a party again.

Almost landed is like being almost pregnant, not possible.

My mind is such a busy place.

Stop falling.

E and Wes jumping on the bed, love this sound.

Abs & E pretending to be twins, lol.

Nico & Vinz = hopeful, good call sis.

I swam with a mermaid yesterday, it was remarkable.

Writing some chapters makes me laugh and writing some chapters makes me cry.

Learned what a foothold is in wrestling, helpful!

Grieve how you need to, to each their own.

3 consecutive plane trips is my max.

The view is on point.

RANDOM THOUGHTS FROM THE WEEK:

There was a dream, remember it!

One day at a time.

E and me are quiet in the mornings.

Next time, call in reinforcements.

Use your head to live with your heart.

Speak truth. Those who recognize it will listen.

Hands in the air when sliding down a giant ski hill on a tube.

Ridongculous...just fits sometimes.

Do your best.

Hiking, now.

French fry YouTube challenge with two twelve year old boys, hilarious.

Gore-tex, barb is so good2me.

Bring a pie, take some cookies.

If you have company and wanna tub, wear a one piece in.

Be kind always, people die and it hurts.

God muscles the sword out, don't wear your arms out trying to.

Jack was a music genius and could make the best silly faces I've ever seen. Hard.

Say yes to the bubble run.

Sometimes I drive in -20 degree temps to eat Amoreena's soup, yes it's that good.

Don't reason with unreasonable.

Aprons x 2 = a good time.

I want to die like Enoch did.

Naps are swell.

Solomon is so my boyfriend.

It's not how big your faith is, it's the size of your God.

<3 kee & deb xo.

RANDOM THOUGHTS FROM THE WEEK:

The show is not more important than the soul.

Pillow fights.

There are talented actors out there, protect your <3.

Kindness is beautiful.

E @ districts & sharing about it over dinner = priceless

Snacks at room 609 and danimals yogurt, youth girls are really fun!

Best way 2 stay out of trouble, the bad kind, serve & be about others.

Some days I miss San Diego more than other days.

We have all been robbed, ripped off, stolen from...be honest with it, God heals.

Mustard seed, basically a speck, of faith, love this.

Play it safe with dating.

Planes always land, just soft or hard...pastor Chris is awesome.

skittle worthy?

Storiesthatteach.com

Sophomore girls feet smell rank, wow.

True friends get it.

Fan of coconut water.

Sheep hat from Romania & alpaca socks from co-op, Wisconsin winter bring it.

Let it go, chaos & the calm, <3. James bay though...

Waffle log homes w/ sausage doors.

Col & Jenni getting married, <3.

Big adventures in store 4 these 2.

Show up & wait for someone who shows up 4 you too.

Work & more work & more work, no way through but through.

Btw you're the French to my fry ;)

Peeps who post uplifting songs on your page, <3

RANDOM THOUGHTS FROM THE WEEK:

The holidays make my jeans shrink.

Goo goo dolls.

Don't try 2 convince someone 2 love you. It comes easy 2 those it should.

Signing books is an absolute blast, I have yet to write just my name lol, hope I never do.

When your globe breaks, buy a new one quickly.

Run the cold off.

Those who can't handle you @ your worst don't deserve you @ your best, Marilyn had this right.

Transparency is salubrious.

When you lose 1 earring, over & over, crud.

Bring socks 2 gym.

For someone who didn't want dogs, I sure love mine.

1 could work 24/7, chose wisely.

Kids are always good, Chels says...that girl is wise.

Pray 4 & laugh with those you <3.

Perspicacious, great adjective use.

Act, don't react. Pray before any of it.

God uses every bit of your past for good, let Him even if it's tough.

Man God brings me will love being in His will, the woods and the ocean.

Turn your mind off every once in a while.

Every work has a num chuck, sometimes several, let them fire themselves if they must but no matter what don't let it be a distraction to productivity.

Church is better without a phone.

Sometimes it takes me a while to find my words & courage but once I do...!

Take a chance. Be bold and live big.

E watches the funniest videos but I <3 when we watch full house 2gether.

ran everyday this week, back in my routine and it feels so good, booyah!

Speak Spanish at dinner, practicar practicar practicar!

Buy dog food, ugh but really....buy dog food.

Some people are not your friends, it's ok to tell them, as needed.

If you care about someone, spend as much time possible with their family.

Friends who help you date smart & make themselves available 4 you.

International phone calls, so cool. It's a big world.

You know 2015 was a great year when working on its photo book brings happy tears 5 mins in...

Chocolate covered cinnamon pretzels from Finnottes & an owner who knows my name, delicious.

Love you texts from family.

E says mom next wedding take Troy, good sign.

Hold fast for better days, keep the faith today.

Andrea proof read these 4 me, she rocks and wears a cool necklace.

Currently on a bus with 200 teens headed to Green Bay 2 love, learn and lean in2 God, thankful!

RANDOM THOUGHTS FROM THE WEEK:

Jeans from Jill, snazzy.

Collector of wine, just go with it.

Sometimes dad is on the roof fixing it thousands of miles away and I feel nervous 4 him.

Don't over think it.

My sister attempted to save someone's life, she is a hero.

Visit dad with Ethan on his birthday if at all possible.

Eating sweet potatoes while in the tub.

Seek with devotion and be ready to respond.

Always wear at least two pairs of socks when hiking all day in the snow.

Make your own tracks but if unsure follow deer tracks.

I'm a natural tracker even if perhaps, not a hunter.

E's high = Michigan won.

Don't miss the God stuff because you're overly busy with good stuff.

If I can't have the ocean, give me the woods!

No one really has bugattis.

Always change your oil on-time.

Highlander is a beast in the snow, <3.

When invited to a wedding, GO invest in magic.

<3 Spanglish, the scene at the end about space is gold.

Welcome to my house.

E and me redid his room tonight so it's more teen, bitter sweet.

Dance!

Make decisions, even hard ones.

Support looks like shoveling snow.

I have a cold, colds are good reminders to rest.

Seeing your children through their friends eyes is a special perspective.

Protect magic.

Work & school tomorrow, pray & show up, it will all be good, come what may.

Romans 12:12.

RANDOM THOUGHTS FROM THE WEEK:

Love waking up with both loves asleep in my cabin...

Tea time, we fancy <3.

The reward for good snow driving is safe arrivals and departures.

Don't work too hard, grumpiness may occur from shear exhaustion, take some time.

Sometimes treating family as you would business and business as you would family is the right approach.

Be open to love those who love you.

I miss Chels already, seeing her walk into that bookstore was one of my favorite moments.

Read the bible in 2015, thankful. Bible.is <3 perhaps I will in 2016 too.

Stay steady.

Horses in the snow, incredibly beautiful.

Pointbreak with E, oh bayee.

Sometimes people argue, it happens, move on and try to be kind.

Kids 1st.

Call dad back.

denise is a fan of my camo yoga pants, so comfy!

Grocery shopping @ woodmans is a good time.

Answer the phone.

Follow your instincts, hug Gretchen.

Kiss @ midnight & in tunnels, cheek or forehead counts.

Blanket they lay over you on the carriage ride is da best.

Sometimes no is the best yes.

Abby is coming to visit me this year, oh my love!

Talk it out.

Salmon being grilled 4 me, delish.

Cancel plans as needed but not too hastily.

Write 2 books in 2016.

Plan big dreams.

Make a date with yourself and don't stand yourself up.

Quick airport goodbyes are better than big fat tears.

Celebrate big, Renee is smart.

No one is perfect.

God is good.

Hike all day New Years.

RANDOM THOUGHTS FROM THE WEEK:

Return containers 2 your friends. If they don't return yours don't judge.

go hike alone, bring your dog.

E is my current world.

Prayer makes mind buzzing stop.

There's something special about a friend asking to take a selfie with you, don't scoff it off.

That look from your friend when you ask her which can soup she used for the base and you know...she made it from scratch. Love her.

Rum extract is very different than vanilla extract.

I am quite serious sometimes.

candlelight services are worth it.

Don't stress over ten minutes on Christmas.

Make the best out of where you are.

Put a cap on your pity party, I recommend no longer than 15 mins.

Strive for bonhomie.

Go be about the good.

Mermaid tails, yes more mermaid tails.

We were going to watch a movie but watched Akaya instead, oh my hilariousness!

Chinese candies always make a good 1st impression.

Genius has a dark side, try not to live there.

Did you know the word courage is based on the french Word, coeur=heart? I didn't, mom but thank you, makes sense.

Navigate the gray.

Breakfast is a meal not a time, good point.

Want to impress, take the trash out.

I'm worth it.

Share your story, tears and all, some people listen & then gain bravery to tell theirs.

Be vulnerable or strong depending on the time and crowd.

The snow is magic.

Time is the best gift.

Going running.

If a Christmas tree is trapped in storage, give it away, giving is its favorite.

Kyle puts Chelsea's socks on for her, I love this fact.

Listen to good music, it helps.

Bring flowers 2 the airport and always give yourself more time 2 get there than you think you need.

irenic tendency is a solid trait.

Seeing Santa at the mall through an unafraid child's eyes is always a magic moment, don't miss it.

Somethings are best kept to yourself.

When someone dies unexpectedly, be extra kind to their family. Hold no stops.

Sugar cookies, steak, velveta, sugar cookies, steak, velveta.

Learn to receive well.

Cry together.

Watch how they handle a bad day, it says a lot about character.

Some do crazy professionally.

When your daughter does your dishes just because she loves you, wow.

Home is faith & people.

I have a headlamp for night hiking, so very awesome!

Your new son in law & daughter saying,"we'll watch E while your major project closes mom", priceless, well worth 16million.

Honor your value and your values, particularly at Christmas.

My sis makes dreams come true all the time.

book reading this weekend, OMGoodness, tis fun! #banauthorwhenigrowup#

My God has a wicked sense of humor.

Carriage ride soon, magic.

Chocolate fountains are harder than you'd think to clean.

Stand up to ridiculous.

Ang says there's just something about an Italian woman making meatballs, love her.

When someone is fighting 4 their life, go love on them & bring chocolate covered macadamia nuts sent from your aunt in Hawaii.

Let us adore Him, while letting Him truly cherish us.

Happy Birthday Jesus, thank you for not staying a baby in a manger.

RANDOM THOUGHTS FROM THE WEEK:

One time I ate a whole bar of chocolate, ok it was Monday.

My girlfriend tells me that my book is too special to be put on a shelf and sends me a pic of it on her coffee table, I love her.

High school assistant principals have the best stories.

Sarah tells me there's a room for me at her house always, she loves me like the dickens, thankful.

By my word may be one of my favorite phrases, especially when carried through on.

Baby Nora is perfection.

I do better when I've had time to think. Internal processor hazard.

Tennessee sunrise.

I'm in love with the word.

Fastest hour I've ever lost was Nashville to Knoxville on 40E.

God is in the waiting.

Sometimes I get blessed so much I can't even believe it.

No love is wasted.

Ok, I actually do enjoy driving in NYC, like a video game but even more nutzo.

Trust your gut.

E's youth leaders came to his last game, no words.

Love that I see horses and buggies regularly while driving.

Sometimes the best thing you can do for a day is have an adventure full of wonder, sans phone!

My my how the seasons go by.

When it's super hero day and we totally forget but E wears a bat man shirt just because, awesome!

Make every second count.

Love with all you got!

Actions speak way louder than words.

Big tvs are overrated.

Chels & Kyle smiled a lot last night, well worth the effort.

Thankful for those who know me inside & out and get it.

RANDOM THOUGHTS FROM THE WEEK:

Being in the future is cool, until you open your work email.

pick one word 4 me, prodigious, not a bad one.

Some days you go ice skating with your new Romanian colleagues. Not many days but some.

bought a sheep's fur hat...smells odd, not sure how I feel about the ethics and why somehow buying it at a Romanian market from an 80yr old woman who could take on anyone feels different than on sax 5th ave, anyhow to rotary lights I go with warm head.

Wake-up.

If you are going to be late, make sure you have some gifts on-hand just in case. Extra points if said gift is hand-made.

Roses are always a good idea.

Chels @ Disneyworld and E @ six flags. Wonder & wind, happy days.

Fairly certain I lose my truck in a parking lot, more than the average person.

The leftover blue raspberry pop-tart that you teased your son about and then ate after dropping him off at school.

When you miss the post office being open by 5 mins, a frown arrives.

Do your job well, forget politics.

Take a weekend for yourself to write in a cottage, or whatever your particular dream looks like.

Long distance loving is one of my learned skills.

In the same breath, e told me I need new dance moves and I'm not old yet, his qualifier is 70 and he actually pointed at a guy on the street to demonstrate what old is, wow, alrighty then.

Alpaca socks, nuff said.

Baby it's cold outside is on the radio while sun is shining on the cabin...loving 2015 winter so far.

Chels 12 days....yes!

Freedom is yours, go do good!

RANDOM THOUGHTS FROM THE WEEK:

Yep, I would have rocked it as a stay at home mom.

I notice that I always think the next chapter to be written is the best 1, makers gonna make.

If you haven't blown bubbles recently, I highly recommend it.

She's 100% all the time at whatever she chooses to do, love this description by someone who is for me.

Stretchy pants vs. jeans on turkey day. I made the wrong call....

Oh sol, let's not be sorry it's over but happy it happened, Seuss is smart!

I brought more books than clothes to Romania...The books are now read and the clothes don't fit me any longer after all the food.

Cheers!

There's something about when your adult child tells you to be safe that blesses your heart.

When you desperately miss your children borrow a baby and get out of the country, but not at the same time or you may be arrested.

This year, all I want for Christmas is a hug. Gifts2 but mostly a hug.

Not everyone says what they mean, be careful.

Feels like magic to hover between the heavens and earth, especially at 575 mph.

Honesty, it's how I roll.

I devour books the way some others devour potato chips.

Dawn's goofball picture she sent, abs & wes's auntie osher video, my bro's lunch date...made my year - thankful.

I told a dear friend my dating rules, she said, I wouldn't date you. I told her good then I'm on the right track. We laughed hard.

The sound of Italian in the Rome FCO airport is a beautiful sound.

There are few places that I have experienced as emotionally charged as the international arrival and departure gates, the love receiving and sending off, so intense, the kind only explained by long gaps of distance entangled with devoted heart ties.

I missed church this week. It's ok God travels with me.

So much food served on Alitalia airline...equal to total amount consumed year to date on domestic flights.

I found my peeps, hugging...waving their arms...Italians <3

Sunshine with a little hurricane.

Romania, from what I've seen, is beautiful. The people are passionate and hard working, also I love the way they interrupt one another...

Bucharest tonight, then cabin sweet cabin with my favorite 12 year old on the planet 2morrow night!

Work well. Respect all people.

RANDOM THOUGHTS FROM THE WEEK:

Catch a sunrise in the sky.

Sad day when I am at TJ's and I can't buy sriracha... airlines.

Appreciate kindness & it generally multiples.

When watching a 20month old, no extra running is required.

Posting thoughts a tad early, Romania, what in the world?! Oh yeah.

Baby got back, dance party with Sol.

Take the long view.

Like my sis says every time during the week Sol wakes up and smiles at me, it is like, "yay, you still here!" :)

Thankful.

Helpfulness is where it's at.

Miss e and chels like the dickens. Love that they are both having a blast!

Naps are good.

Thankful.

Flippant than entitled is a bad combo.

Poop happens.

Sometimes it's best to just throw a blanket over your head, close your eyes and call it a day.

Thankful.

Funny thing the heart, once someone lets you in to their world and you let yourself care for that world, it lingers after they close the door on you.

Strong back bone and healthy funny bone are key.

Delivery of 50 hot cocoa & 50 hazelnut somehow = 150% when thoughtfulness is added.

The children's museum is a good time.

Friends who invite you into their home when your kids aren't with you on thanksgiving are the best kinds of friends.

God is good, all the time.

Be thankful everyday.

RANDOM THOUGHTS FROM THE WEEK:

Hiking in the mist.

Come to church by all means, just can't sit by me, that's me & the big Guy's time.

Sometimes you ask a stranger to tie your sons bball tie and he is kind and you feel like the best mom in the world.

100% carrot juice, just how I roll.

There is nothin' wrong with free tires, 1 for all 4wheel drive, oh yeah!

Little boys grow faster than we can catch them.

First book 4 sell shortly after thanksgiving, ahhhhhh thankful!

E cleans-up good.

Run even if you forget your socks.

Asking for a horse drawn carriage ride through rotary lights a month in advance is a good move.

Hard 2 pick, I love watching e play but watching him cheer his buds on...close second.

I miss Chelsea! No one snuggles like that girl!

Do not escape to Tarshish.

It's official, I love boot socks.

Stretch 2b magnanimous.

Eat the donut.

Magic exists, most people rush right by it though.

Superhero niece, yep no surprises there.

Dancin' with bubble wrap on the floor, I have some good ideas.

Youths who hurt, hurt my heart.

My amazing sis and amiga's birthday, there just aren't even enough flowers in the world...

Sometimes when e isn't home I eat popcorn and carrots for dinner.

I get asked on a fairly regular basis what drug I'm on, not sure if this is a compliment or put-down.

Support the dreams of those you love. Never be a dream crasher.

Me & Sol, Sol & me. Grateful. Love thanksgiving.

I am a cloud surfer.

Met a new friend in the o'hare yoga room, she lead me through a YouTube work-out, good times, no stranger danger in a yoga room.

Jess says, "I just can't wait to see her face!" <3

Whatever u like, we do 4 you!

Give hope the chance to float up.

In 2009, your girlfriend will want you to meet her love @ a foo fighters concert, go! Someday you'll be in their 1st year memory book waiting to hold their baby girl.

When watching hope floats, during the dancing father/ daughter scene, you'll have to call your dad if you still can.

RANDOM THOUGHTS FROM THE WEEK:

Run hard when it's time to run, then rest hard.

welcome friends to your town in style.

Many prayers have been said in grocery store parking lots, be ready at all times.

Wizard of oz is on the tube when e doesn't feel great, just how it is and I love it!

When you have had a major life change, make sure to bring tried and true friends with you, while meeting new friends who can hope for you in a past-less way.

Mauka state of mind.

Sometimes a friend brings you an entire pie, just because you liked one piece..cherish good friends!

compliments look good on me, or so Kel observed.

E thinks ortho and dentist appts in one month count as the same and is not a fan, he has a point.

I killed a mouse!! Eeeeeekk

My friend found my bible, I almost cried! Feel like myself again.

Try new restaurants and always be kind to waiters.

Nice is nice.

Banter is the creamer of life, so sharp.

I get to hug Jess's belly in 5 days, oh WOW.

Ruthlessly eliminate hurry, speed is overrated.

It's taking e going on vacation without me 4 a week 4 me to get snapchat..we do what we must. Chels is proud of me 4 being on there, lol.

Turkey & gravy chips....?

Big time players make big time plays. Football learnings with e.

Sometimes one adventure is going to Iceland & the other is staying with Sol.

We're fighting from a place of victory not for victory, this perspective makes all the difference.

Take the chance.

pretty hard to sweep off my feet with all that residual lead.

Live big.

What did I do before having 7 seats, so flippin fun to listen to e and his buds!

when it's time 4 work, work well.

Magic needs to be protected, my brother is wise.

Discernment is 1 of my peeps.

One on one with Ethan in the kitchen, slick moves, boxing out! nothing better!

Lioness rising.

Just a whiskey glass if you aren't making a toast.

Have a bit of landloper in my blood.

Transylvania and Romania Union celebration, 19 days, wow can't make this stuff up. Note 2 self, bring garlic.

All in or all out is a good way to be!!

Another sweet peanut coming into this world that I get to love on, this is a really good day! Must get south soon!

I could get used to having a driver.

Power forward in action, love my boy!

God carries me everywhere.

Mighty random book proof, oh my goodness gracious!

Sweet package delivered to my girl from my Gretchen :).

Given one choice - horn or gps for driving in NYC, pick the horn.

Superman has nothing on me.

eye souvenirs Trude likes, I like Trude.

Bacon and salmon are delicious together, I did not know this.

If you're going to night hike, bring a lantern & prepare to be amazed.

Friday night in the Boston airport is like a meat market 4 the overworked, geez.

When the lady sitting next to you offers an Oreo, the answer is always yes and cheers, yes we tapped our Oreos...

Judge not, lest ye be judged. Love instead.

I get to drive my bro & sis's subi!

Courtney & I need to live in the same zip code.

Piggyback is the only way to cross the finish line.

I fundamentally disagree with wasting food.

In the kingdom, hope = certainty.

City of refuge, yep.

Some people were born to be Sunday school teachers, Billie Sue is one of these people. She also taught me it's perfectly ok to wear long dangly earrings hiking.

If I only had one helmet, I'd give it to you Chels, buckle up big day! Love you!!!

RANDOM THOUGHTS FROM THE WEEK:

Chocolate covered cinnamon pretzels for breakfast.

Kind words and actions heal hearts.

My brother and Rihanna, love it!

Matthew west and Francesco concert whoohoo, good choices count.

I am not very photogenic because I laugh so much, which I don't mind I'd rather be loving life than just look like I am.

Hello by Adele, enough said, so good!

Views are worth hikes, always.

I write better today than yesterday.

All about the execution.

Decide what you want to be, then go be it.

My hairdresser calls me his day maker, I like that.

They call sun roofs, moon roofs here.

When you wake-up and Cass texts, are you Wonder Woman today? Instant smile - Day is made before you're even out of bed, lol!

First 5 mins in Wonder Woman costume, I stepped in dog shizz, about right...

Learning how to buy songs on my phone might actually be the most awesome 2015 learning for me, no offense masters.

Some people are passionate about supporting you, let them in.

Chels, I am movie splash zone, enough said. Love her more than words can say. Best of me.

Any holiday without your boy is tough.

Mindful people don't try 2 control others.

Mill worms are surprisingly wiggly going down.

Be done with pretending.

The cautions of a discerning friend are a gift.

Raise 'em up.

How is it possible Gina is 12, she's magic! <3

RANDOM THOUGHTS FROM THE WEEK:

Sunsets.

Lamaze class, kicks, fighting to breath, good morning cooing, babies are miracles.

be. YOU. tiful.

Love those who remind you 2 fight 4 yourself.

Peace found.

Chelsea's ring bearer puzzles, oh my cuteness!

E's hugs are priceless.

Chapter 5, learning to live without anger. Perfect.

Being late without a good reason shows lack of respect.

When fear is not present, anger does not arise.

Psalm 37: 3-4, delight.

Show your son the work you are proud of.

Give awards.

Abundant grace.

Act old later.

Abs is a bball tourney champ.

DC2 challenge equals 48 hours no Social media equals nice.

God is in control.

Landon is a good bowler, noted.

Freedom is not free.

Think forward not backward.

RANDOM THOUGHTS FROM THE WEEK:

62 degrees.

Squeezing my dad extra tightly next week for Jean, and her dad.

and then, pidgin died.

E is drinking straight from the Brita which seems to defeat the whole filter purpose.

Perpetuate a blame free culture.

Eagles for days.

So many people fighting cancer, ugh, prayers.

Chels facetimed six times yesterday, love her so!

Audi, Barb and Cheryl all in the same day, so blessed!

Walk with momma T, complete with green eye shadow and lotion, lovely.

Golden eagle dinner. Boy Scouts, prepared. For life.

curry, chicken, coconut soup.

An hour at the children's museum is a good time.

Take the high road.

Be humble.

Text favorite recipes.

Be goofy.

RANDOM THOUGHTS FROM THE WEEK:

My own teeny bottle of essential oil blend - joy, peace & happiness, now that is a sweet 1% friend.

Ca = remember when

Wi = now

Wa = tiny home dreamin'

Kingdom coach.

Jujitsu.

Giving freely requires great trust.

Love (agapao) is to will the good of another.

Families 4 peaceful tomorrows, our grief is not a cry for war.

Boyle heights love walks.

What a great God she knows.

There is no pride so dangerous, so subtle and insidious, as the pride of holiness.

Audrey said I remind her of Juliet binoche's character in chocolat, made my year.

Some wrestling parents seem a bit off their rocker.

Me, myself and I.

Scratching Chelsea's back as she goes to sleep, <3!

The best thing 2 hold on to in life, is each other.

Shinrin-yoku/forest bathing.

Cola's face when she sees her leash.

In n out!

Sam hunt education by Chels.

Make the world feel small.

Do the best you can.

Bubbles.

Sneak peak into ft Lee, cool.

Allegiant.

Run & rest everywhere you roam.

Pt. Townsend is someone I love's calm. Breath deep.

Doctors, pain, legs.

Pray.

The humble man whispering the answers to the top dog after researching them 4 hrs, so the team looks good, yep him.

Love, love, love.

New totem 4 J, Matt watching.

Dad said his birthday was super, enough said.

Tappin' Chels in.

E homeawayfromhomework.

Zoo & picking Kyle up from the ship.

TGICalifornia.

Grace dances and work never ends.

RANDOM THOUGHTS FROM THE WEEK:

You are my sunshine, my only sunshine.

Moms doing dishes.

Fire fighting 4 Al, Matt watching.

Flamingo 2.

Wild at heart.

Polar bears, I see why they're his favorite.

Ang & me, impromptu sleepover.

Love isn't ever wasted; got to hug log, em, Ju & col last night.

Knox is smart, love that about her.

God smiled on me when He gave me Caroleann.

Chels is a love!

Give yourself time with new things, never done this before.

Grocery shopping with and for dad.

Sunshine is laying on me.

Healing is good & hard.

October 25, 2015 was a good day.

When your <3 is right, your words are right.

Matthew 6:33.

Complain to God, he can take it.

In twenty years will I want him to remember a morning with grandpa or Disney, yeah Mickey can wait a couple hours.

Ang & Chels taking turns, my <3 is lighter.

Wild Indian, uncle cliff was right about me.

Trust your instincts.

E says, "that was nice" I say "which part?" He says, "all of it."

Read 2 your dad.

Life Goes On.

Can't imagine the pain of losing a baby, prayers.

Disney Magic, indeed.

A thrilling alpine adventure.

Waiting in lines is seriously cool quality time.

Be a person of your word.

Marble Halvah is one of my favorites

When your daughter

& son in law make you and E Easter baskets. <3 I love Easter.

Pray for the Potts family.

It's my papa Maza's and sis Sarah's birthday, I love them.

RANDOM THOUGHTS FROM THE WEEK:

Be there 4 those you love; anyway you can be.

Teeth...urg, my bridge & Aussie licorice had a fight.

10 days Abby oh yeah!

Chels and Yoda hold hands in the morning.

Keelee's coming!

Don't worry.

Isaiah 41:10

James 5:16

<3.

Confirmation is a beautiful thing.

Wow that was a morning.

God is good all the time.

Don't forget to breath.

Make the decision that will let you sleep well at night.

Be good 2 u.

Talk 2 your boy.

Proud of Chels.

Brave.

Chia seed your soul.

Push forward.

Sometimes it snows a lot, have I mentioned I love my garage!

Miracles in heaven movie date 2night, oh my.

I love my tribe.

Hug babies so tightly, and old people, and everyone!

Fly wheel.

Raviolis requested by E.

I love Easter.

RANDOM THOUGHTS FROM THE WEEK:

The beauty of being with people who know you and love you year after year.

hair salon magic.

For such a good listener, you have really small ears.

Love it when E leaves his basketball in my truck and it rolls around, makes me smile!

Some guy without a shirt sat next to me on the 2 rowing machines. The rowing machines at the gym are too close together.

Faith is the only true shelter.

Soul on fire.

We get there when we get there.

Miracles are everywhere.

Stop the glorification of busy.

Soft fabric clothes.

There's just something about having a pineapple in my shopping cart that makes me happy.

Put one foot in front of the other, repeat.

Baby Linda ultrasound photos make my day.

You're my sunshine.

Best friend, medical store, heart of gold lifting my worries, nuff said.

Support is incredible.

Go hiking.

Slept by Bella on the couch all night, sweet girl.

Do your best in your heart.

Be there 4 the tough stuff.

Hold-up a true friend with both hands.

No matter how small a footprint, it can make a lasting imprint on your <3

Need more hymns in my life, bought a book, almost stole one from service but that seemed a poor idea.

If I must be buried, bury me under a beautiful tree like that 1.

Paint a canvas, bring your picnic basket and enjoy every second.

Think globally, act locally.

Sam makes one good Cobb salad.

I <3 Easter, e comes home today @ 4, can't wait!

God is good, all the time.

RANDOM THOUGHTS FROM THE WEEK:

Scars don't go away but they don't stay the same either.

King of my heart.

Chels sends the best jokes 2 me and seems to know right when I need 1.

6 months flew, yeah sure u betcha.

Buddy may have outgrown the kennel, promising :).

Move your dna.

I ain't got no room in my bed...I ain't got no room in my head...hoots & hellmouth, oh yeah.

Wear some purple on Easter kind of like on St pattys with green ;). Also, don't wear a watch.

Restraint inspires restraint.

There is no humping allowed at Asha's house. Benji 2 buddy, darn straight!

Easter love, raviolis, raspberry cheesecake.

Pickling in the kingdom together.

Geshmak!

Call me any cognomen, as long as it's a kind 1.

When you feel yourself emotional about something, wait, pray, wait, respond. Saves apologies and helps 4 good sleep.

Evening hikes, yes please!

I see kayaks on roofs, oh yeah!

I smell like a Bon fire, by far it's my favorite perfume.

Really trying to remove the word hate from my vocabulary.

I'm good in emergencies, it's no accident.

make decisions with integrity behind closed doors and it's much easier to maintain your integrity when the doors open.

To be known is a gift.

Run.

Breathe.

Pray.

RANDOM THOUGHTS FROM THE WEEK:

Keep the end game in mind.

Life is rubbing elbows @ the community table....hmmm.

Loving the word welp....

Ice in a baggy and bandaids are magic for booboos.

Souls desire 2b understanding. Ego desires 2b understood. Shoot for the 1st.

If you love 2 dance so much you can't even stand it, message me.

Few things as fun as driving 4 boys 2 youth.

Beloved.

Drive-in movie theatres.

Charlie won!!!!!

Believe God for big things.

$ave dat money.

Izzys 19, what! XO

A new mixer for my girl, be still my heart.

Life is a classroom. Chose your teachers wisely and study more than you think you need to.

Some love going 2 the dentist, proves there are all kinds... personally I prefer crowns on my head.

New York can be wild.

Thankful for you, yes you.

Green fielding...the people I work with are rad.

Grow or go.

Work, work, work.

Friday night lights, evening hiking bring the headlamps!

We pick up Abs tomorrow, yes! She has my heart, her cousins head, hugs, kisses, wonder and granola.

RANDOM THOUGHTS FROM THE WEEK:

Dogs out, welp.

Let the 3 year old take the picture.

Good people get on well.

Respect people who carry children up and down mountains.

Hike higher than you plan.

Kiss your boy, pray with him and let him listen to his music.

Sometimes I am so happy or sad I must speak in emoticon pictures!

No one really wants 2 pay bills, think bout it. Say no to stuff!

BellaGoose = beautiful lead.

I will rejoice in the simple gospel.

Costa Rica coffee and Audrey <3.

I'll lean not on my own understanding.

Flyover America after driving to msp and jetting from Seattle.

My niece is lovely & fun.

Brevity with critical conversations is key.

Pizza studio pie.

My house is ab's alarm, good taste.

Favorite key chain & granola, ohana.

Run, rest, repeat.

Shoot for the moon.

Shell yeah.

Nederland is home to lost boys like me and lost boys like me are free.

Waves and dance party on the docket for today!

Free days = bliss.

RANDOM THOUGHTS FROM THE WEEK:

Catching snow flurries on our tongues in a hot tub, magic.

Cousins have the coolest bond, good friends these 2.

Even when my faith necklace isn't on, it's on.

I <3 being an aunt.

Sometimes Ethan tells me I love you multiple times when I drop him off at school, today was 3x, <3 <3 <3.

Birds are chirping, sweet sweet sound.

I miss you more than the wolf misses the moon.

People before profit.

Finnottes & Root note with abs, <3.

Slow mornings are the best kind.

It's logical.

Boast in God.

A full house makes my heart smile.

Whatever you are at the moment, be the best one.

God of the city.

Replace the word shame with grace and carry on.

Help each other.

Unbelievably pro-active.

First in, last out.

Dating yields vases.

I figure pay for good food now or medical bills later.

Contretemps and me happen.

Lean and dab.

Live in hope.

Fry an egg.

Take a sweet boy to the museum.

RANDOM THOUGHTS FROM THE WEEK:

Get over your bad self.

Yes I have a children's museum membership. No I don't think its odd.

Say no to crazy, again.

One day working per week is a divine ratio.

Giggle freely.

Every dead end leads to a new discovery.

18,850.

That one extra postcard from Tennessee that you have......

Sometimes the answer is to howl.

Ugh.......ok I feel better now.

It is possible to put too many chocolate chips in pancakes, I was mistaken.

4 seasons in 1 day = Wisconsin.

She's everything. Good song, glad he sent it.

It takes time to be creative. Slow down.

Give yourself more time than you think you need.

Bake your friends cake shaped like a heart.

Leave love notes in the forest for your friends!

Love your neighbor.

Exodus 33:14.

The bare necessities.

Abby loves taking shuttles, who new?

Incorrect grammar hurts my ears, I even correct it in songs when I sing.

Always bring a book on a trip.

Love big those who love you.

Happy sibling day to my brother, <3.

Waterton canyon, bootyful!

RANDOM THOUGHTS FROM THE WEEK:

I belong in the mountains.

Agave & tijuana.

namby-pamby people are not for me.

Introvert or not. Talk with the person on the airplane next to you.

Learn your friends worlds.

Watch the sunrise from under the covers.

Eat good food.

Hike.

Fb says Izzy is my bff, smarter than it looks.

Colds stink, so does missing my last dc2 class.

My sis loves my book and what I wrote to her, Jackie thanks for funding the experience, <3.

Awe the beautiful bellies growing and first time moms glowing.

We buy more McDonald's during monopoly time than we do all year! Something about it that lights up e and me.

Great friends take notes for you and send prayers via text.

Mars will come to fear my botany powers!

Ethan prayed I feel better tonight, <3.

I'm buying The Martian, E knows good movies.

Sick stinks, me so sleepy, going home after noon meeting and snoring until I pick up E.

My boss said I sound horrible, nice.

A get well bag 2 my cabin, <3.

Chels and her grandmas are good, blesses me.

I feel better in her Green vest.

Be proud of your friends being successful always, lift up whenever you can.

50 years, definitely someone 2 celebrate. Sweet song for a sweet team member.

How are you song? ;)

Time, time and more time.

Love hearing chels voice.

Call my dad back.

Lost boy is such a great tune.

Make goals, align them.

Empower smart people.

Out of office 4 2 hours.

Tired...sleep...pu E, then share with youth. Thankful.

RANDOM THOUGHTS FROM THE WEEK:

Cupcake on a fasting day, put it in the fridge quick!

Ethan calls me and the pups, "hey fam". Love this.

I worked both dab and fam into my youth talk, +3 for me!

Treasure old friends.

When you're speaking for youth and your boy and his friends sit front and center to support you, nothing like it.

T loves kites :).

When's it's time to follow, follow. When it's time to lead, lead.

He won't lead me where he doesn't go.

Hebrews 6:19.

2 miles ✓

Chase the wild dreams. Run like we won't run out of time. Live like crazy. Love me baby. Are you with me?

Pure is power.

I have one child who never wanted to go to school and one child who never wants to miss, go figure.

Soccer is back in full-swing oh yeah!

My niece practiced with the us rugby team & sent us the kindest thank you card, she's one cool chica.

hiking & kayaking are in my future.

done, not fair but done.

The best things are free, my girlfriend is smart.

God is in control. Trust him.

I love when Ethan hangs over the back of me when we're grocery shopping.

7.

Thankful for the sunshine.

It was a burnt cookie miss the sunset kind of day but I also got a piggy back.

Good thing I have two scrabble boards. Buddy ate one.

Not another minute.

Facetiming Chelsea at 2am makes me have a better day, but hiking at 7:30 is gonna hurt.

Chin-up buttercup.

RANDOM THOUGHTS FROM THE WEEK:

Hike. Hike again.

Joseph's life, study it.

When truth presents itself, the wise person sees the light, takes it in, and makes adjustments.

The fool tries to adjust the truth so they do not have to adjust to it.

6 hours on the soccer field with E, <3

This field is big.

PSALM 112:7.

I have a girlfriend who rides a motorcycle to meet @ javavino, cool!

My daughter says I'm her hero, taking that to the bank 4ever.

When life is hard, rock babies. If you don't have 1 find 1. Nursery workers help.

Serve, it gets you over yourself.

Shoot 2 the root.

Beat the drum with me.

God always provides.

Lots of people love us but at the end of the day, some days we are in a room by ourselves. Pray & act with integrity.

Sometimes people surprise you, other times they don't.

Be there for those you care about and their children. It matters.

Radical faith looks differently on every 1.

I will always like photos of green fields smelling of hard work and & hope-filled future crops.

2 work I go, thankful for able hands.

Tithe no matter what.

Sleep is good.

Go to dear friends birthday parties, especially surprise ones!

Tuck E in tight. Tell him the truth always. Love him every minute.

<3 Rigs, Pray.

Life changes fast.

Hold fast with endurance and patience.

Pick up your side of the log.

Next chapter & college for Ethan.

Focus.

Tractor ride on bucket list getting closer to completion, yahoo!

RANDOM THOUGHTS FROM THE WEEK:

Sun is shining.

Foolish pirate, the treasure is hidden in my <3 not chest.

Be where you need to be.

Make the best of it.

Cinnamon toast mom, yes absolutely!

Difficult roads often lead to beautiful destinations.

Love my nephews, every minute.

Every girl wants 2 b fought 4.

Slow your roll, lol.

Today would have been 20 yrs, it's not. End of a long book. I left it all on the mat, 2 kids are magic...next book.

Instagram - ok work peeps, come on over.

The high road is not on most maps, use a compass.

Where exactly is Ibiza?

So sleepy!

E plays music all the time, love this.

Oh how I've missed you IHOP on Tuesday nights @ lcc, whoohoo!

The River is beautiful.

Oranges in the morning remind me of my dad.

Keelee is coming eeeekkkkk!

Smelling more flowers tomorrow. Goals.

Lowering his shield & taking a knee. He's a warrior.

Nurses are tough on the outside & all heart on the inside.

Carry a blanket, pillow and food in your truck, just in case.

Joe's home on D's day, God knew.

Pups are guarding me, sweet pups.

Am so having a Bon fire Friday :)

Chels knows just when 2 FaceTime me!

RANDOM THOUGHTS FROM THE WEEK:

Some drink, I write.

There's an easy way and there's the right way, not the same usually.

Sometimes I leave the dogs out and it rains....for hours. Egad!

So glad it's not yesterday today.

The reality is out of 1,000 people, 1,000 people will die. True story.

Romans 8:6

Cable, ortho, dentist

Coffee with Audi and Tea with Trude, blessed.

Garbage barges on the river honk sometimes.

Team building event for RE student support on the river 4 20 mins, heck I'm in - heels off!

dress barn, really? What a name.

17 hrs today, wow am I glad Ethan had a birthday sleepover planned. Great team.

Driving a tractor and shooting a bow, whoohoo! Bucket list progress ✓

John 8:36

Prince falls.

Manners make things better.

Run outside instead.

When experience warrants, stop talking with fools.

See the differences between wise, foolish and evil people.

Cross country skies and bread maker from my God momma and beautiful night filled with Roy and Nancy adventures!

Photo caught while dish washing.

Dragging main in Wyoming <3.

Door knob 4 a kiss.

Hike with barb = power 4 both of us.

Knox checking up on me. <3

Coffee dreams.

2 Tomah I go, soccer time!

Miss chels deep in my gut.

Billie sue's texts make me smile.

RANDOM THOUGHTS FROM THE WEEK:

Hope.

Cards from Carole just when I need them.

Listen.

Tithe with faith, even in uncertainty.

Beauty out of ashes.

Wes lighter 1 tooth. Nothing like the 1st.

Don't judge.

Armless crawler.

Make every second count.

Ponder it in your heart.

So many chills, loved Tuesday night at ihop. Beautiful adventure and treasures.

Hug and pray big!

Technology war rooms that include success cookies are a good time.

36 million people enslaved in human trafficking around the world, whoa.

Olympic flame in Rio, Solar city tower, wow.

Celebrate generosity, don't envy accumulation.

Plan ahead.

Love well.

RANDOM THOUGHTS FROM THE WEEK:

Do life together.

Mom's portrait of Bill & Anna. Love his head on hers <3.

Sex Esteem looks different on different folks.

Worlds largest office party, seems unlikely.

Chai mix in my bake sale brownies, why not?

Gonzo.

Keelee in my tub <3.

Hebrews 12:28-29

Chocolate macadamia nuts, delicious!

Be here now.

Few days as special as this one.

When someone puts his hearing aids in to be sure he hears every word you say.

Fixing the flowers of her first husbands grave = heart.

Sugar and spice country store.

Long ago lane.

Guideposts.

I love driving trucks!

Grandpa Lew says there's no music but country music, lol. He also said if you make a mistake thats ok we all do but if you don't learn, & do it again, that's dumb. Cheers 2 the second.

Grieve the way you need to.

We do better when we know better.

Sports Ngine.

Watching Ethan play even while freezing on the sidelines and drafting outage messages is still a good time!

Hot Cheetos & cookie dough ice cream kind of night.

The boys & buddy....oh wow.

Setting up a tent in the rain, love that E.

13 - 18 = blink of an eye, even when busting my butt working in WI.

Miss chels like the dickens.

Love him with all I have...thankful 4 a certain miracle boy who plays with my hair. Happy birthday baby.

RANDOM THOUGHTS FROM THE WEEK:

When a Starbucks manager/youth leader brings your boy a treat that requires extra effort, it makes you all smile.

Sing happy birthday over ice cream.

May Day.

Carrot cake w/ nutz for the momma.

simply take no time 2 worry, life flies.

Run.

Take your family hiking.

Hebrews 13:16.

Egad! Cavity 4 E...crud.

My auntie Deb is beautiful.

My cousin is good people. She wrote these words on my work wall.....admiration, gratitude, silliness, deep heart. I love you.

Picked up Abby and my pottery treasures. Beauties!

Dad in sept, thanks aunt Vic & Kay <3

Savor every moment.

Feingold in the neighborhood.

Chels and Kyle are a good team.

1st error found in book 2 in record time, it's all good. Thankful for a voice.

Wes muds & Gina sings.

Vulnerability & precision don't necessarily hang in the same crowd.

Perfectly cooked Hamburger @ 9pm. Yum!

Last youth night of the year, it's been rad.

Work in Atlanta 2morrow, bring on the learning, grits & Anderson, Avett, O'Malley hugs!

Micah, Court & Dawn bday love!

Praying flight is smooth & dare I say even early 2 get me back 2 my boy Sunday!

Love to all the mommas, awesome honor & responsibility <3.

RANDOM THOUGHTS FROM THE WEEK:

Budget challenge to the int'ed degree.

Cows out 2 pasture.

Going 2 see Billy Elliot, whoohoo!

Big farm equipment reminds me of transformers.

Create value.

Know your North Star.

Lean into the things that are working well.

Hard times stink.

Good friends trust & know you'll reach out when you're ready.

Dark draped hotel rooms even when working are cozy.

Reward talent and effort.

Invest and believe in yourself!

Meeting new smart people who used to be strangers!

When Ethan says I love you twice at the end of our calls.

What I write, I own, love that fact.

Couch chats with small cute dogs is just as sweet as with large cute dogs.

Long walks & talks.

Linda pearl...spirited yellow, YES!

Love much, speak gently.

Mule eating corn.

We all fall down. - Avett can play!

I'm a super mom.

About 3 more randoms for mighty random 2, then all good, next book time.

On the phone with my mom, headed 2 my boy, reading texts from my girl, loving this particularly happy momma's day!

RANDOM THOUGHTS FROM THE WEEK:

When you are tempted to be sad, bless others instead.

Surprise might be right around the corner.

Hug tight.

An ounce of prevention.

I'm oenomel.

The power of the other.

Self rescue swimming training @ 6 months, cool, can't hurt.

Mother's Day miracle.

The strength of the pack is the wolf, the strength of the wolf is the pack.

You be the sun and I'll be the moon.

Unworkers stick 2gether.

Each time I plan a Bon fire, it rains, go figure.

Wait 2 see if people's words and actions align, then adjust.

Pray.

Good thing I'm not a shopping fan.

It's ok to be sad. It's also ok to be happy.

If you only have 2 minutes to talk with someone, be extra kind.

Play bball in the street.

Help find misplaced children.

Love big.

Rock with your girl on the porch.

Listening to chels and e wrestle makes me smile.

Enjoy time to talk with your sis, even if you're under the covers.

Cards vs. humanity.

Breathe Ash breathe, aria come soon.

Drive safely.

Good men wear aprons & plant roses on Mother's Day.

Office smaoffice.

Research more than you need 2.

Treasure great cpas professionally & personally.

Talk or sleep all night.

Bible & story time.

Summer is just around the corner.

Her children rise up and call her blessed.

Thankful.

RANDOM THOUGHTS FROM THE WEEK:

Choose to shine.

Momma bear will come out if one messes with my loves.

Loving every single 1 of my 38 years.

Only treat the gospel as gospel.

Run and pray, many times at the same time 2 b lean.

Kids know much more than we think they know.

Be honorable always.

Haiti next month.

My girl is incredible. Love her more every single day, watched her board a plane just now, wanted to keep her next 2 me 4ever.

E likes when I pick out his clothes the night b4, love this fact.

Obviate today 4 tomorrow.

Mow someone's lawn, it makes their day.

Be more creative than it takes to curse.

Happy nurses week. Blessed to love & know a few important, amazing people with this title.

Work smart, save every penny, enjoy now, hope for then.

Celebrate.

RANDOM THOUGHTS FROM THE WEEK:

Chai.

Honest pay for honest work.

Be there for the command dinner.

Nurses in San Fran, <3 <3 <3.

Two soccer games. Can't even wait!

Parenting is a verb, barb is wise.

If I have a bad attitude, put me in the woods 4 a time-out.

Soccer with snow in May, wow.

Cut the cord already.

Wild thing was a blast, we owned those rides.

Drop from 207ft, ✓.

You know when E goes to sleep at 8:30 it was a full good bday present day!

Grace upon grace.

Hemmed in.

Used my book proceeds for our valley fair tixs, 0 now, so worth it!

Tyler loves to acumn, Gomez household has some clean floors.

Centered.

You are not a copy.

There is an actual bird's nest inside my house, from the woodpecker's work, Karen says its called mutualism. Cool & not cool, all wrapped up into 1.

Free yard waste dump in the town of Campbell, who knew.

E helped a lot.

God is good all the time.

20 days til Haiti.

Best lawn, no expertise, thankful.

Isaiah 55:8

RANDOM THOUGHTS FROM THE WEEK:

Hips hurt I hear.

Sat in my reading room for 2hrs tonight & read, take that tv in the corner!

No is a complete sentence.

Sow seeds.

E played piano for Nancy & Roy, it was beautiful.

Coming by 4 a visit is a treasure.

Chels <3.

Maintenance is hard 2 maintain.

Psalm 23.

Dentist, crud.

Psalm 29:11.

Miles make accidents especially hard.

Once your baby always your baby.

Sunset chasing with Denise.

Boat 2 Colorado.

FaceTime'ing in the hospital, better than nuttin'.

I work with some high quality people.

Yurt 116 has my name on it.

Nothing better than campfires.

Pinewoods fan.

If they make you a pb & j and write your name on it, they're good people.

RANDOM THOUGHTS FROM THE WEEK:

We were born to boogie.

Electricity.

Sometimes I sleep horizontally, just because I can.

COLOSSIANS 2:2–3.

Do your diligence, some reports are furphy.

Sagacious, not bad mom, thanks for the compliment.

I love that when I tell Chels I'm going to play bball with her bro, she says 2 be safe, lol.

When you decide on financial injustices, go gain some perspective.

Logan is graduating, no single place I'd rather be than there. Those who can be, show-up 4 him. His heart is gold.

I see a light, it is the end to dogma.

People don't belong in boxes.

Pure creates clear thinking.

Love finds a way.

Breathe deep and pray hard.

Somedays I drive to westby to make boys spice pancakes 4 dinner, hug their dad and climb boulders @ a park.

Teeter totters are for adults too.

Occasionally I get tired of being strong each day, I cry, then remember how big my God is and how my friends lift me up. Thankful.

T minus 1hr until my boy is home.

Sunsets and bridges bring smiles.

Eat fruit.

Love my Chels.

My brother and I both love Billy Elliot, weird.

Pray with those who call you.

Don't hug brides so tightly.

RANDOM THOUGHTS FROM THE WEEK:

Hope.

<3 to the moon....& back, no time 2b stuck on the moon.

Nick & Eric, they do, :).

I choose you is the foundation of any solid relationship - 4 faith, friends & family.

Laugh hard.

Psalm 67.

Fight piper fight.

God is good all the time.

In times of strife, a friend for life.

Turn! Turn! Turn!

Tis a gift 2b simple, Tis a gift 2b free.

The sound of the rain reminds me to be still.

I like making E's day.

Micah's girlfriend, happy day!

Learn how to say, when.

Compassion, kindness, humility, gentleness and patience. That'll do.

Observation: On my E weekends, my phone use drops significantly.

Zootopia.

Don't go chasing waterfalls. Courtesy of Saige, fire!

Approx. 1,673,481 cows, wow.

Graduation overload.

Even maggots need 2 eat.

Don't break your arm patting yourself on the back.

Take the river less traveled.

Colossians 2:6-7.

Chels is smart.

My sis sends me photos of the woods, it's like oxygen.

RANDOM THOUGHTS FROM THE WEEK:

Birds in the morning, 1fav thing.

Buy cards with your boy 4 people you love, send them with him to your hometown.

Proverbs 20:21.

Done, heavy but done.

Cooking me meat is a good way 2 get me to like you.

When E doesn't finish his captain crunch, it's my pleasure to.

Waste not, want not.

Galatians 5:1.

Ft McCoy adventures complete with sirens.

Stop for ducklings.

Doughty doesn't sound like what it means.

You are still alive, don't forget it.

Complaining is a trap.

I'm such a bad rester.

I love my friends who ask me the tough questions.

Safe, kind people rock.

Rotary cuff, ouch. Not 2b messed with.

Proverbs 31....She is clothed with strength and dignity. She can laugh at the days to come.

All tickety-boo.

Weaning off wifi.

Cheap thrills.

Consult docs, trust God.

Chels & Kyle with my dad, no words, all <3.

Pain is distracting, physical or emotional. Fix my eyes.

Take a sip, turn a page.

Dairy days, soccer, dinos, Haiti.

Weeds or seeds, tough 2 tell @ the start.

I will not tease Chels for loving this couch ever again.

Phil 4:12-13.

Elated is a good word.

Sciarra.

RANDOM THOUGHTS FROM THE WEEK:

Free.

New friends.

God always has a plan.

Injustice is relative.

where's your passport, sweet boy.

Jezi renmen ou.

Blow your horn.

Pastor Asha, way better than apostle.

2nd cor 4:18.

Can't unsee what ones seen.

Re-entry brings baggage.

Eat plantains not salad.

Choose to be led in worship like David, don't worry about any one else.

Dance @ church & restaurants.

Love big every day.

Keep your nuts.

Jump out of shower when your kids call & log on to FaceTime.

Use your horn when go-cart driving through Haiti.

Bible for Jean David & Anne.

Baby smile for me that I'll keep 4ever.

Sleep soundly on a stranger when your sweet heart hurts.

Learn languages.

Good welding, good heart.

Swim.

Get baptized in the Caribbean if you can.

Sing.

It is well.

Upstream. Find the source.

Stay up to watch sunrises.

Time 2 work in a different way.

Flowers on the counter, fixed water pump = love.

I can do things you cannot, you can do things I cannot; together we can do great things. Mother Teresa.

Think before speaking.

Touch heals.

Be in the spirit.

What is happening? Lol!

Last random, mighty 2 out in fall.

Haiti 2 heels, deep breath.

Love you.

Printed in the United States
By Bookmasters